Merry
CHRISTMAS

This Books Belongs To

....

....

....

....

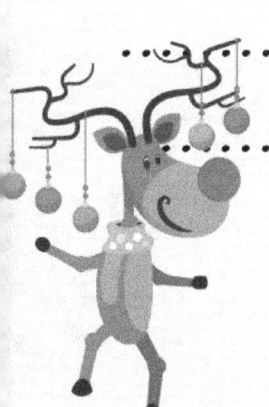

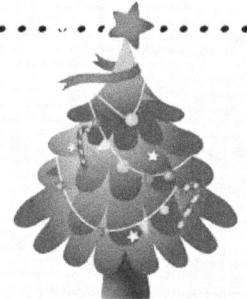

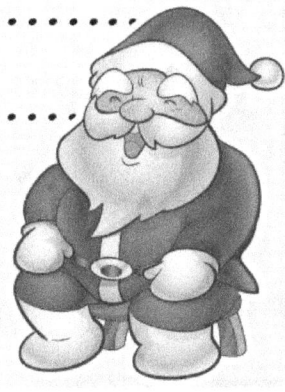

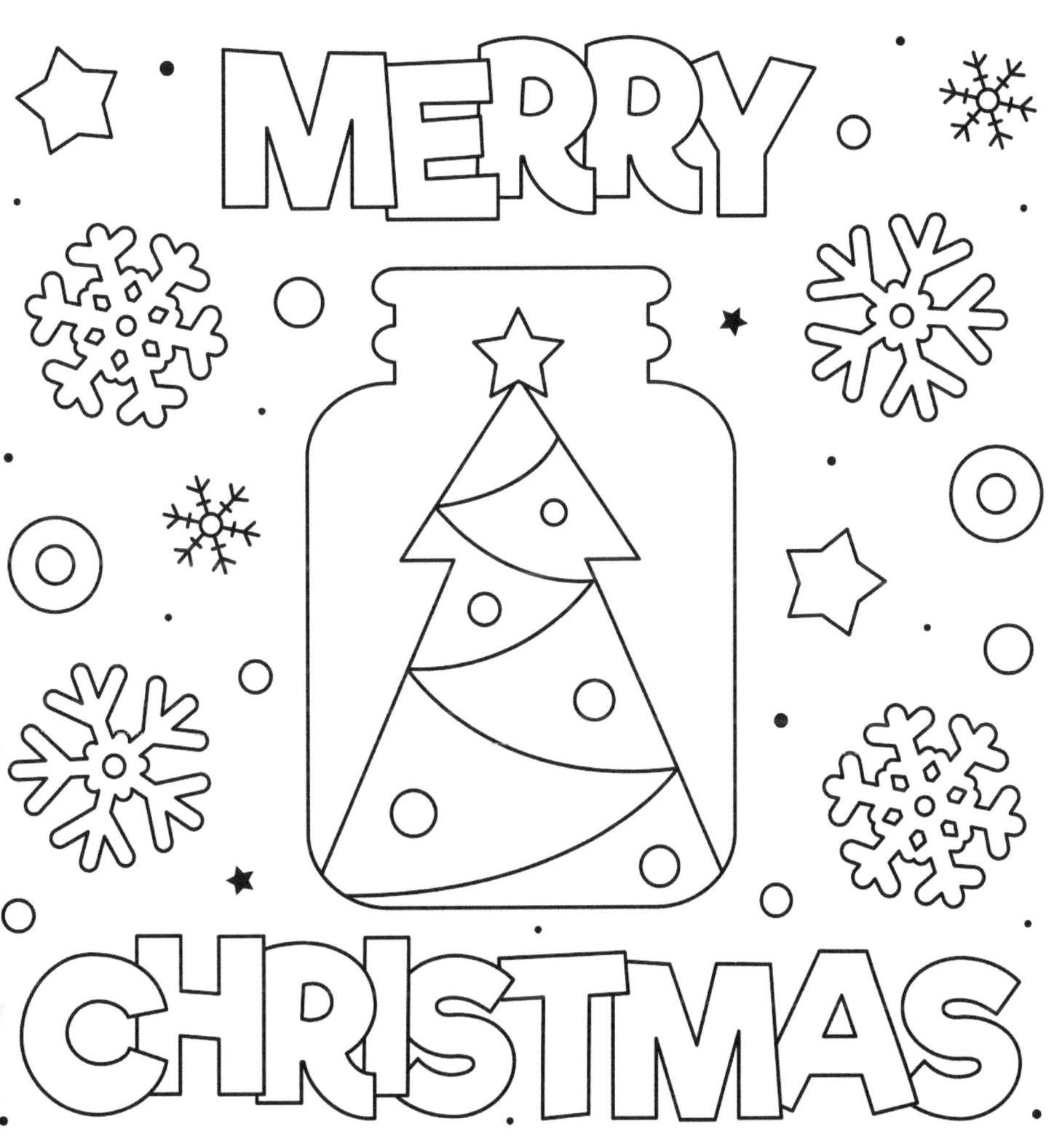

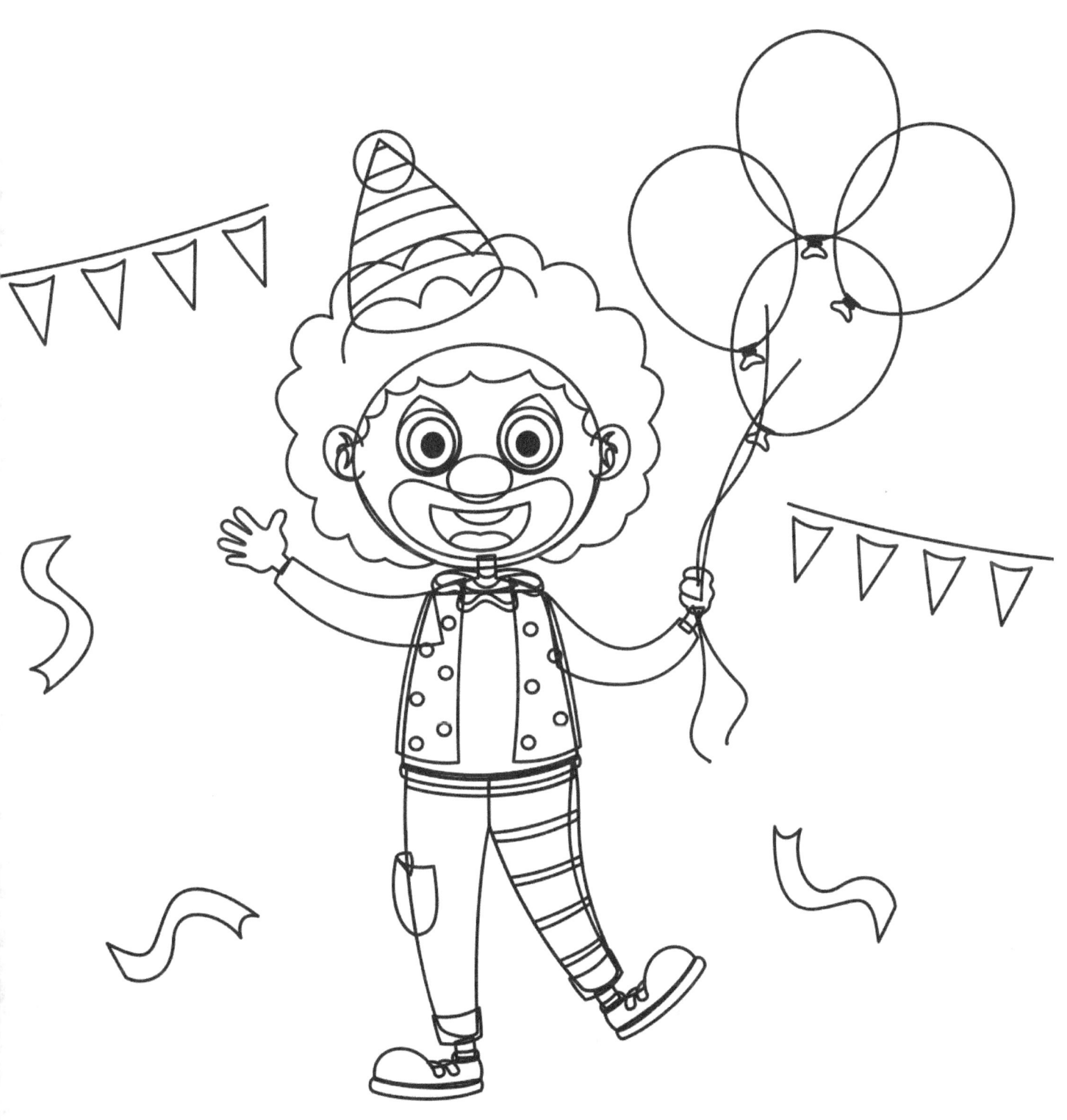

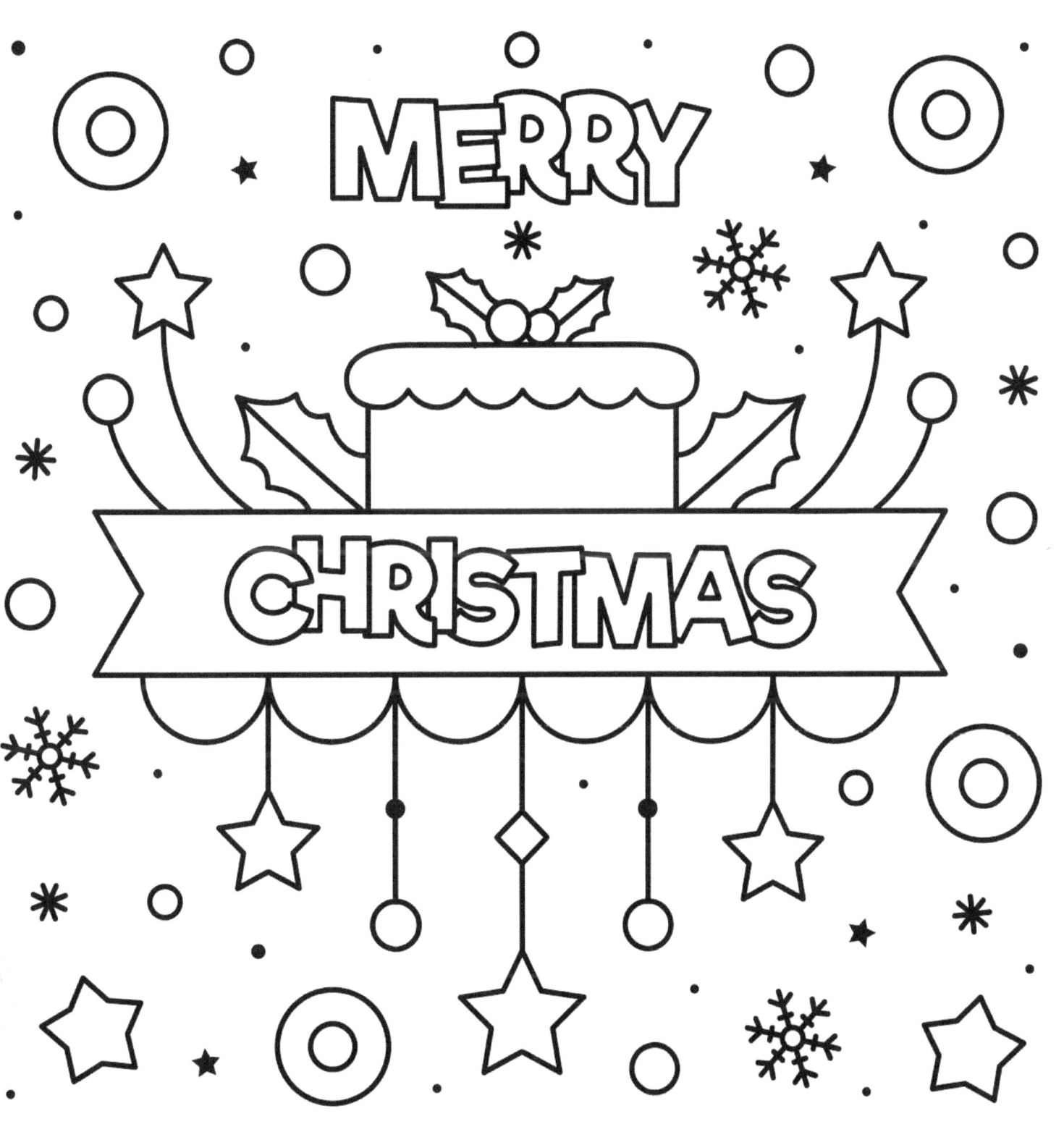

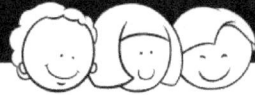 

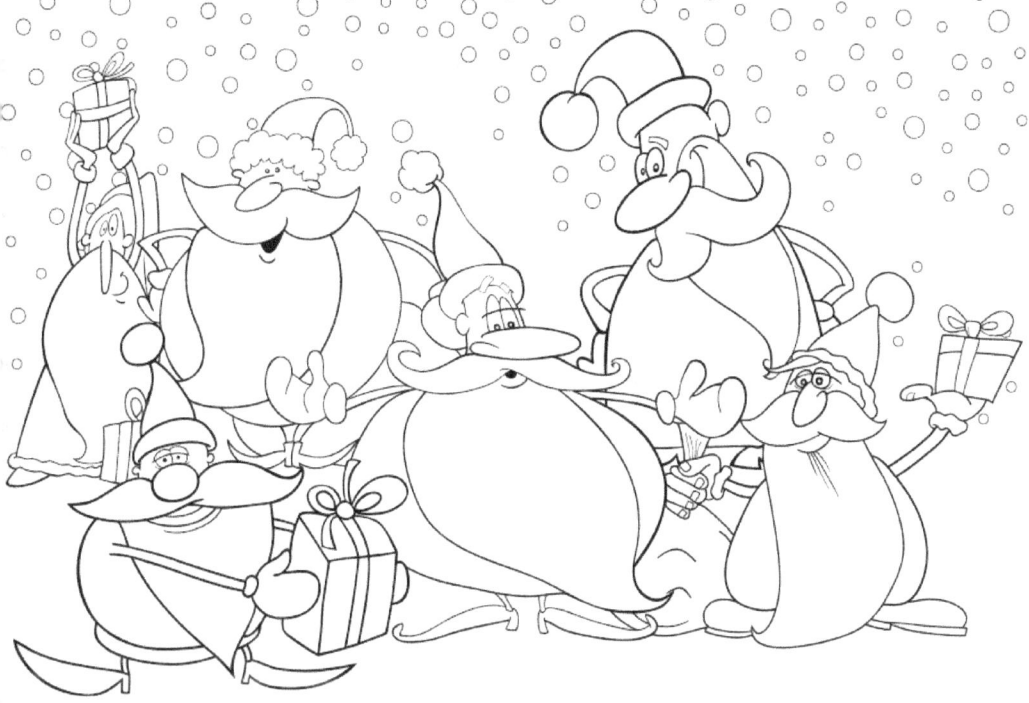

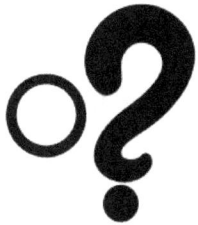

FIND
7
DIFFERENCES

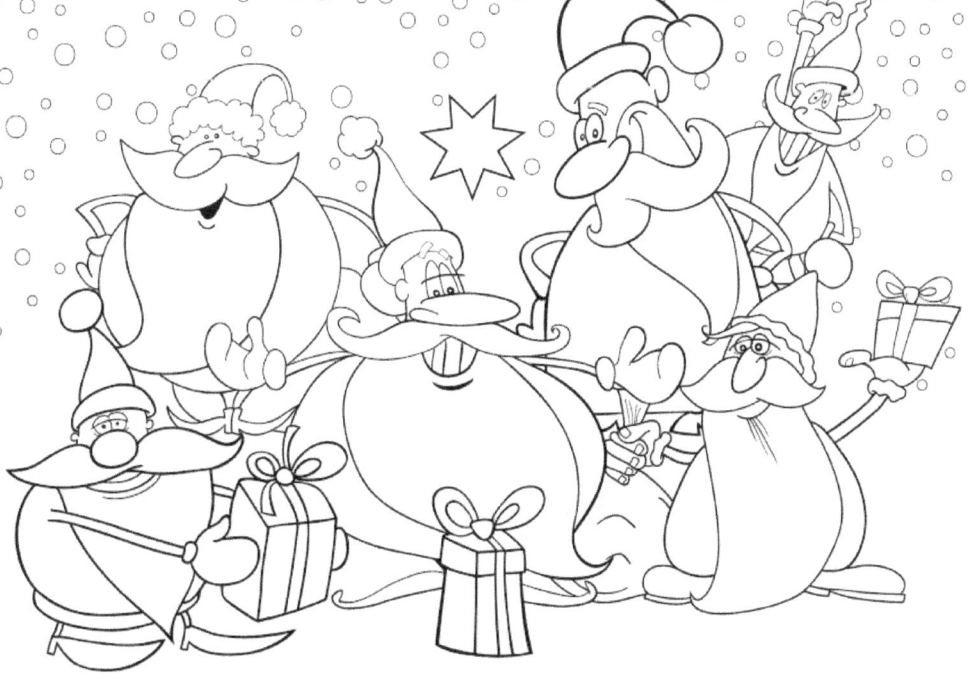

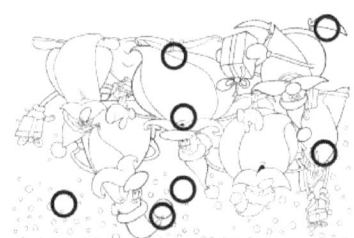

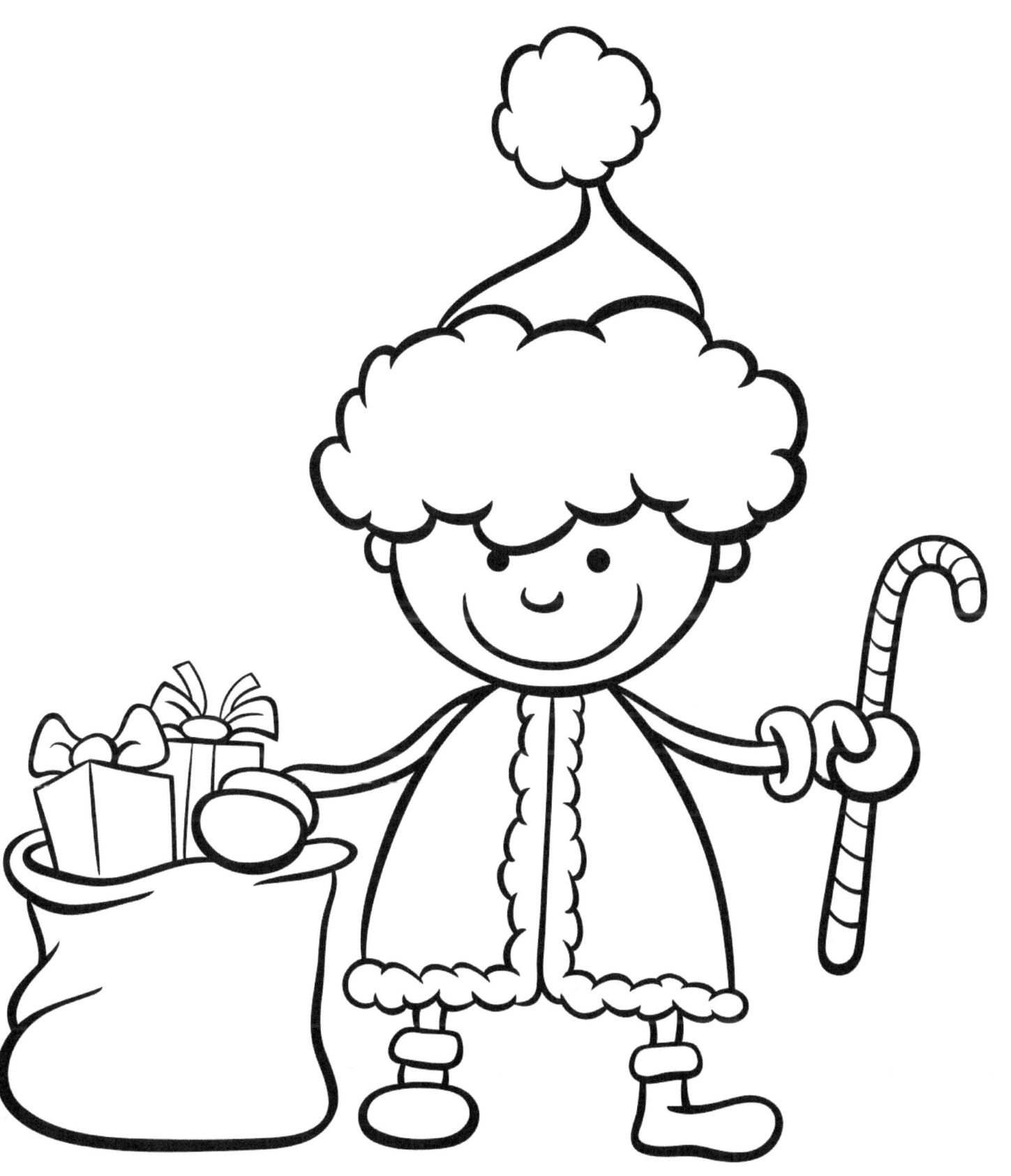

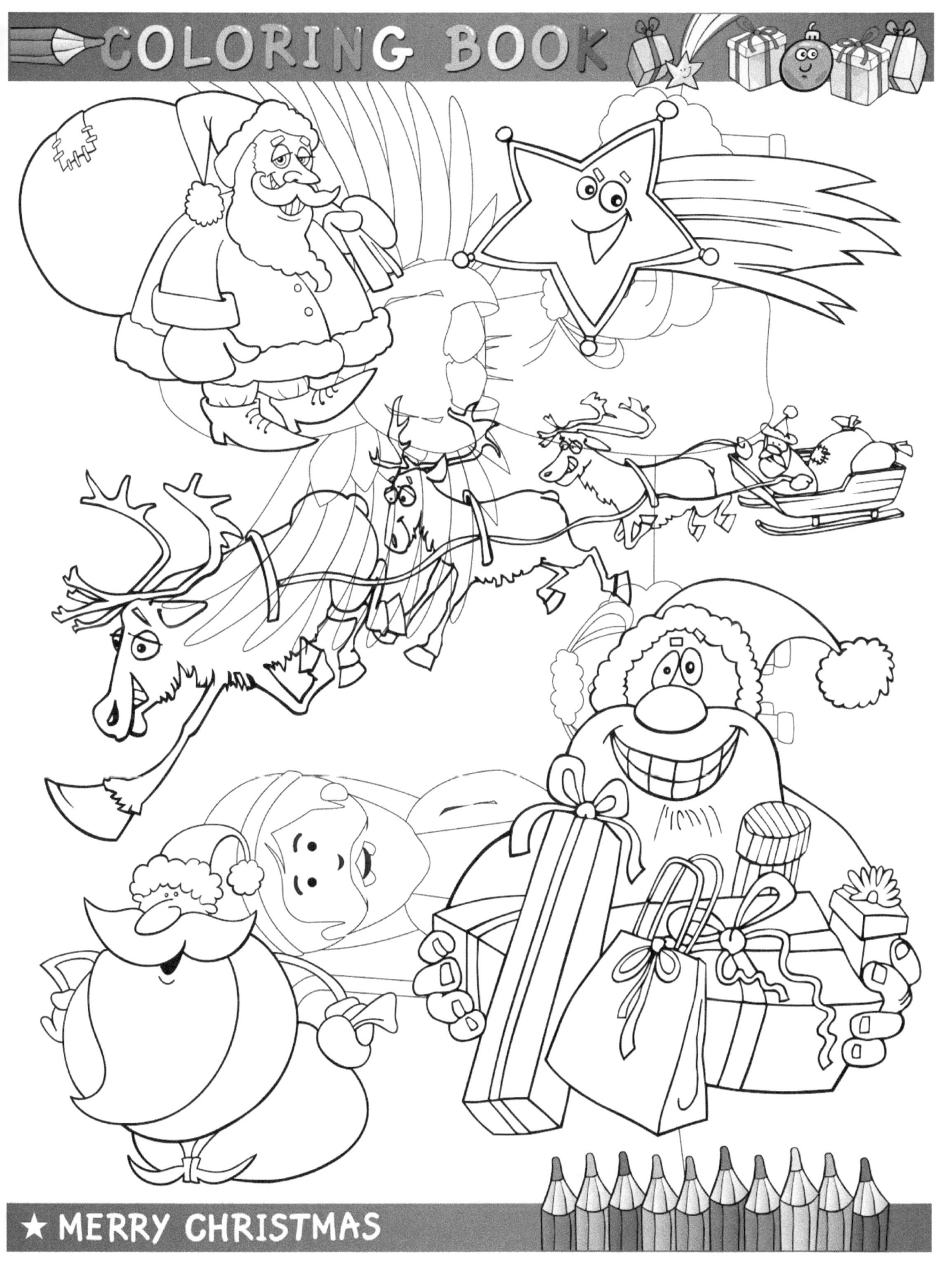

COLORING BOOK

★ MERRY CHRISTMAS

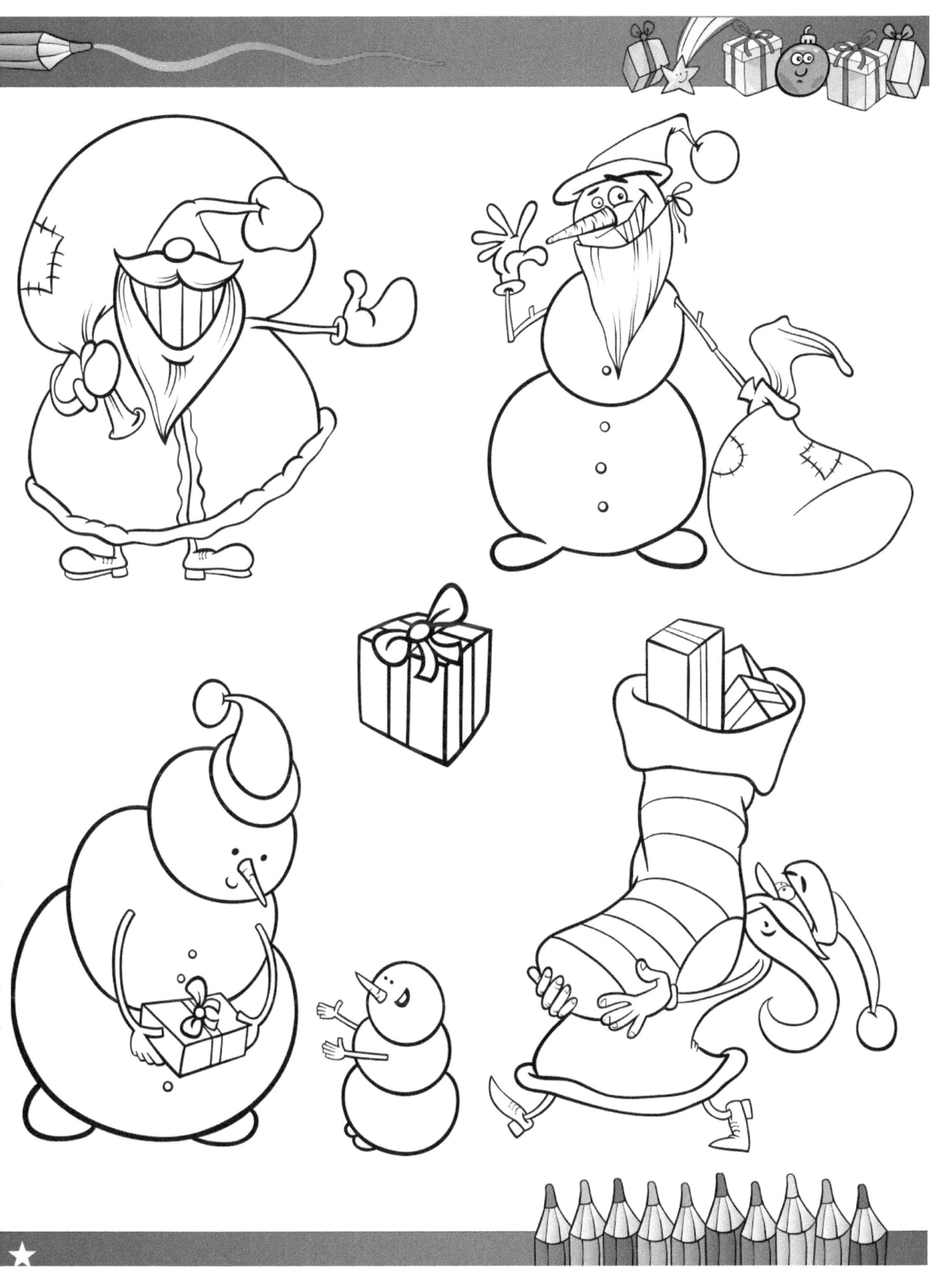

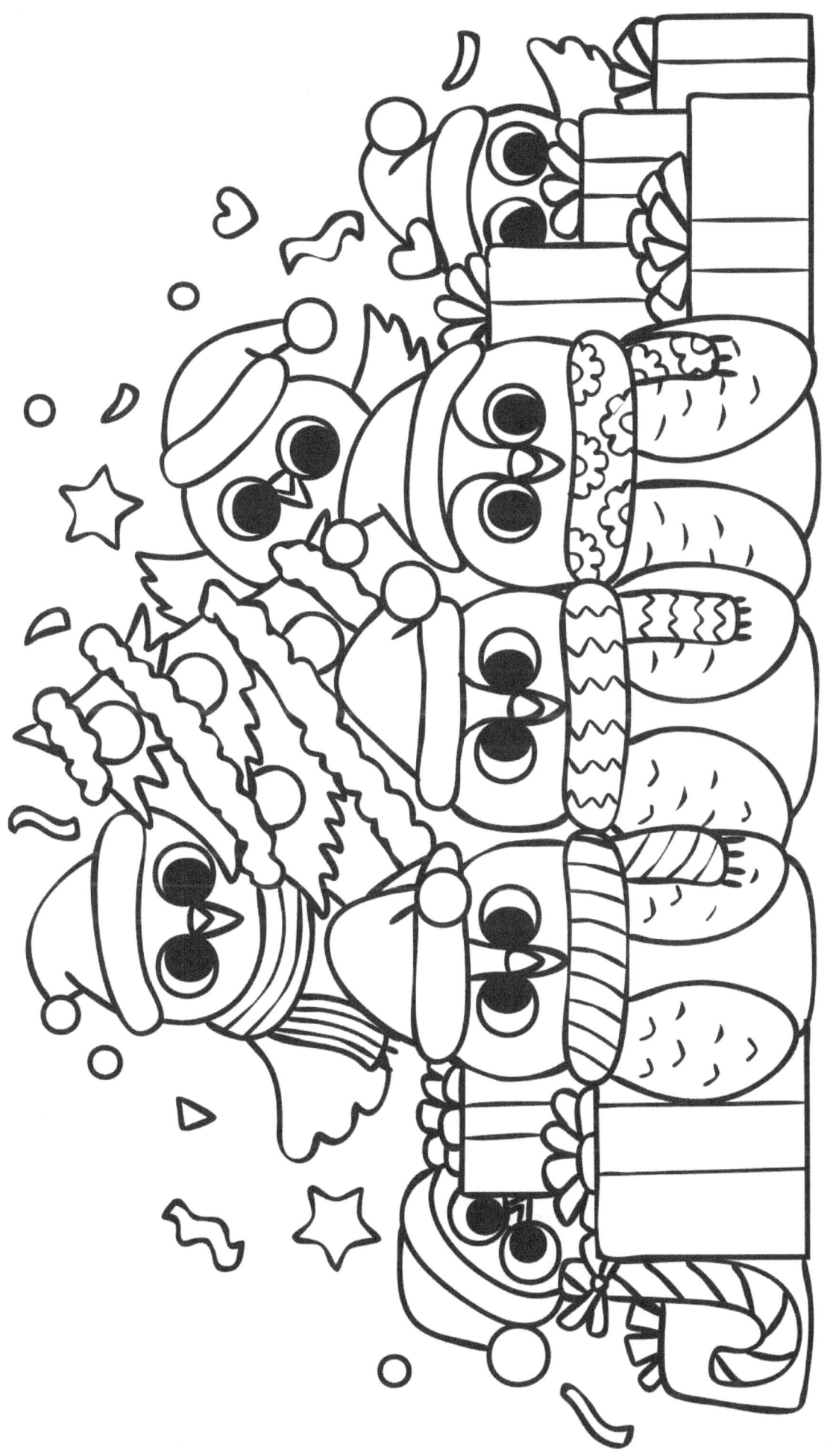

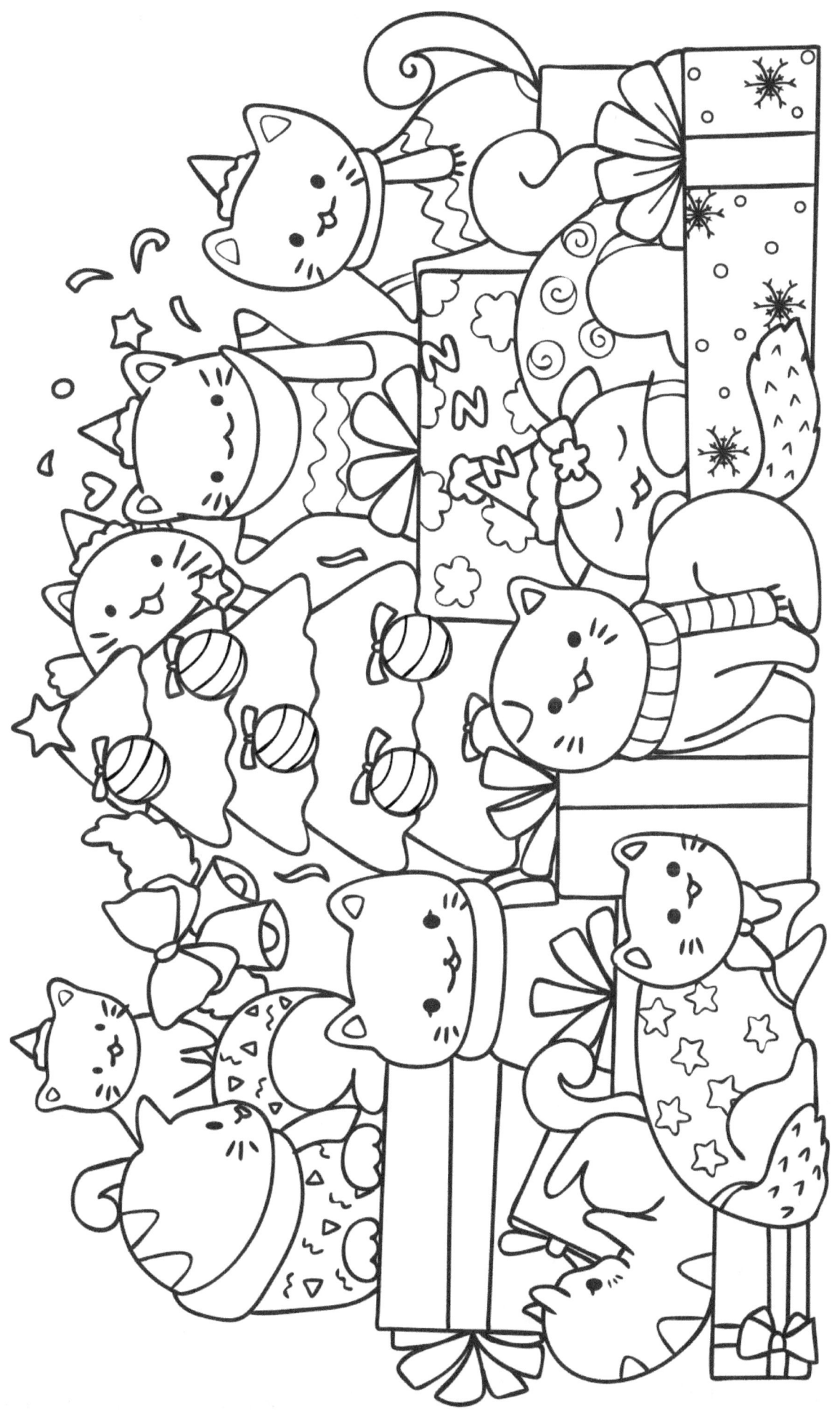

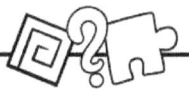

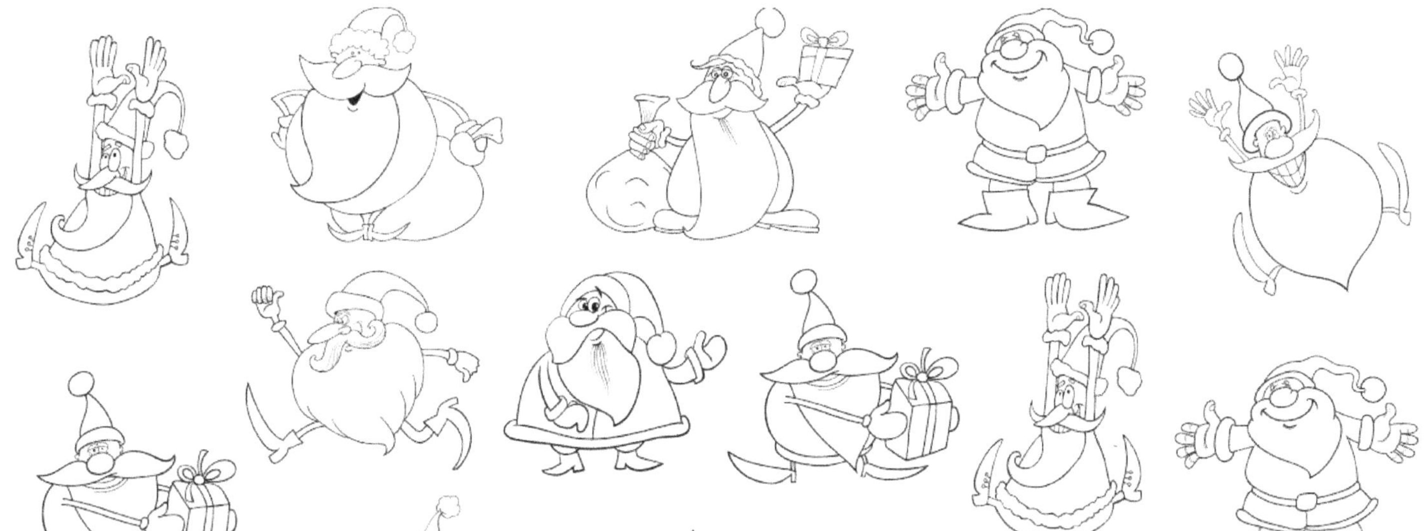

CHRISTMAS

FIND
ONE
OF A KIND

ANSWER

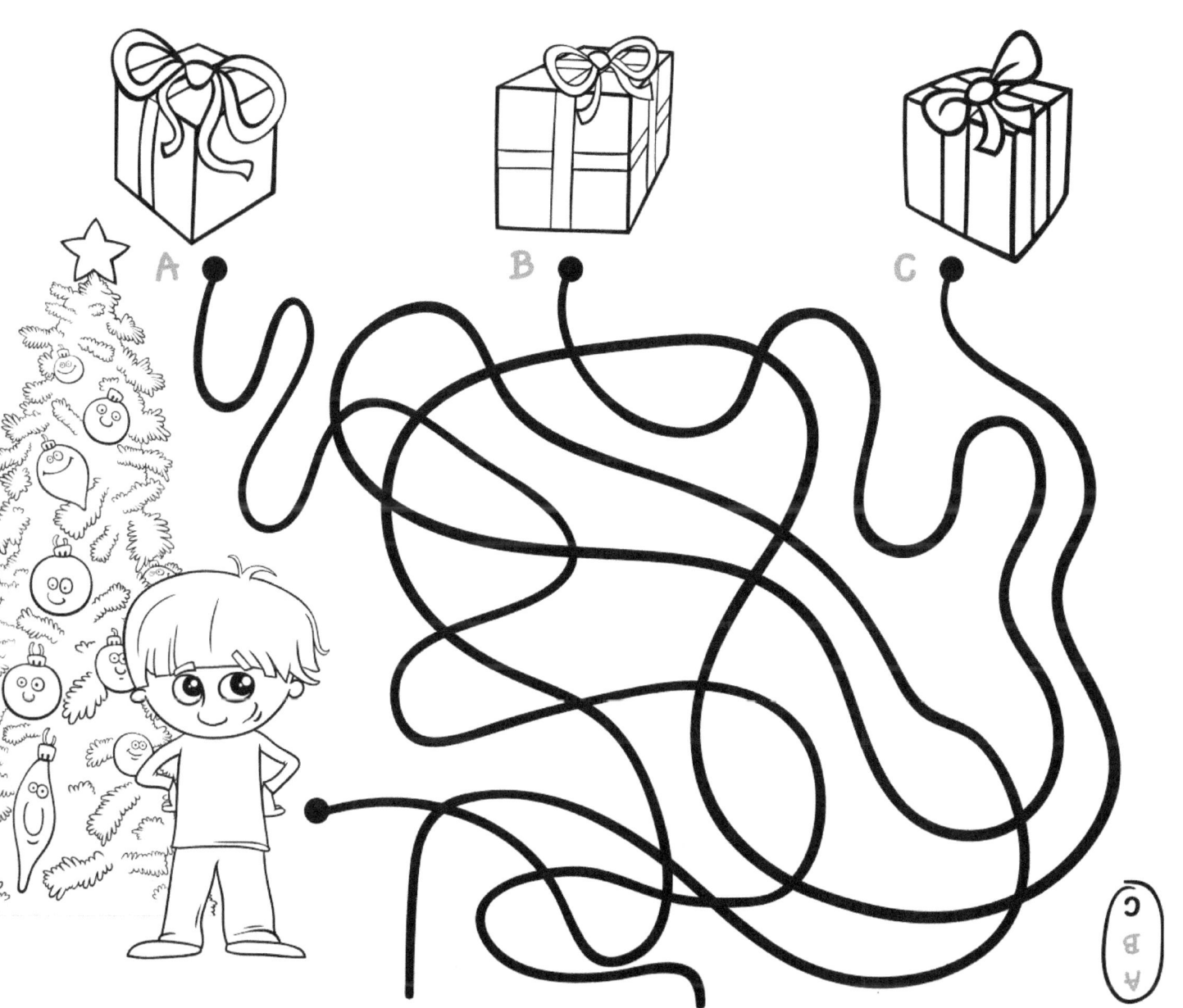

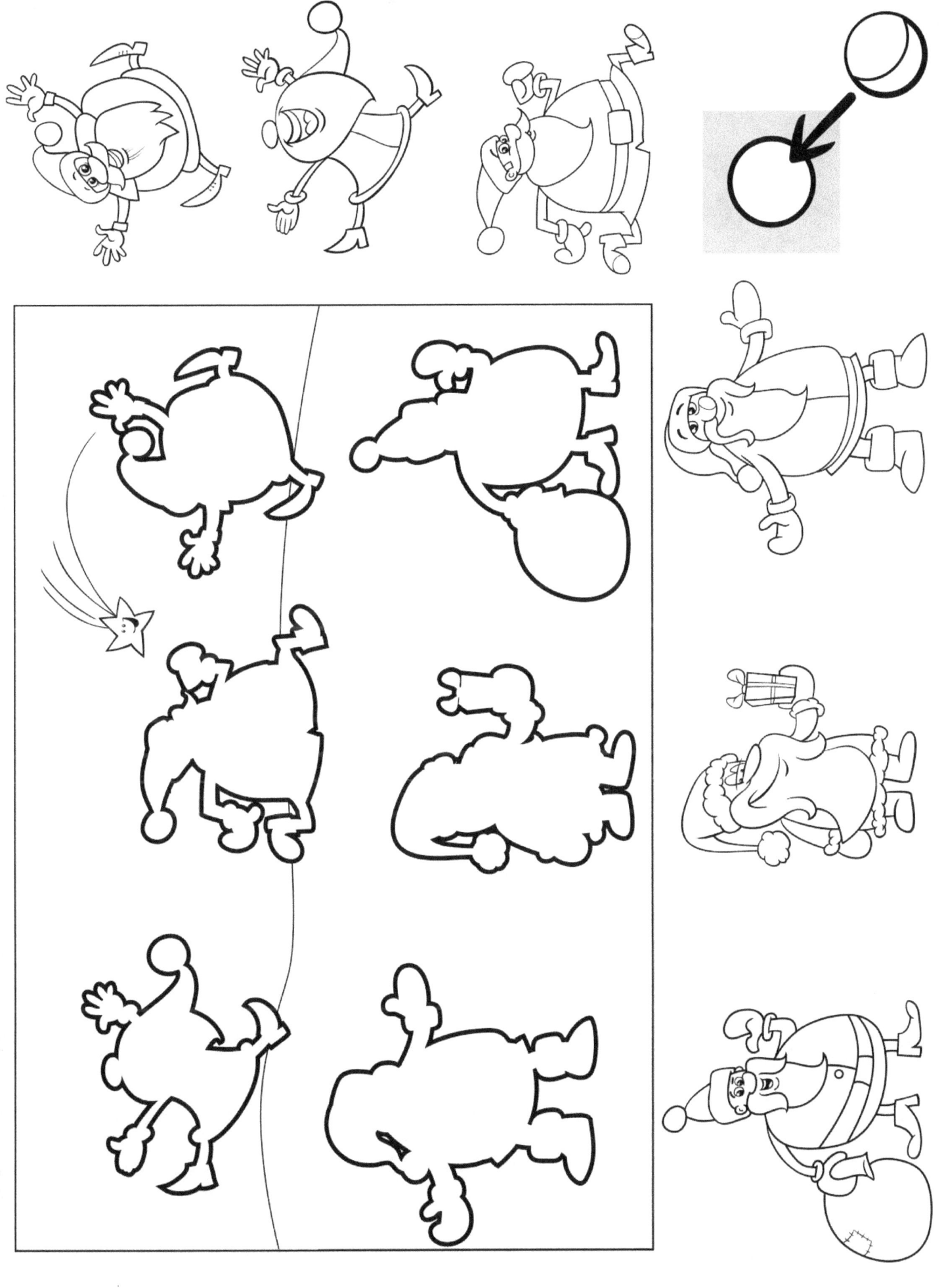

WHAT COMES NEXT?

ANSWER

1			
2			
3			
4			

1

2

3

4

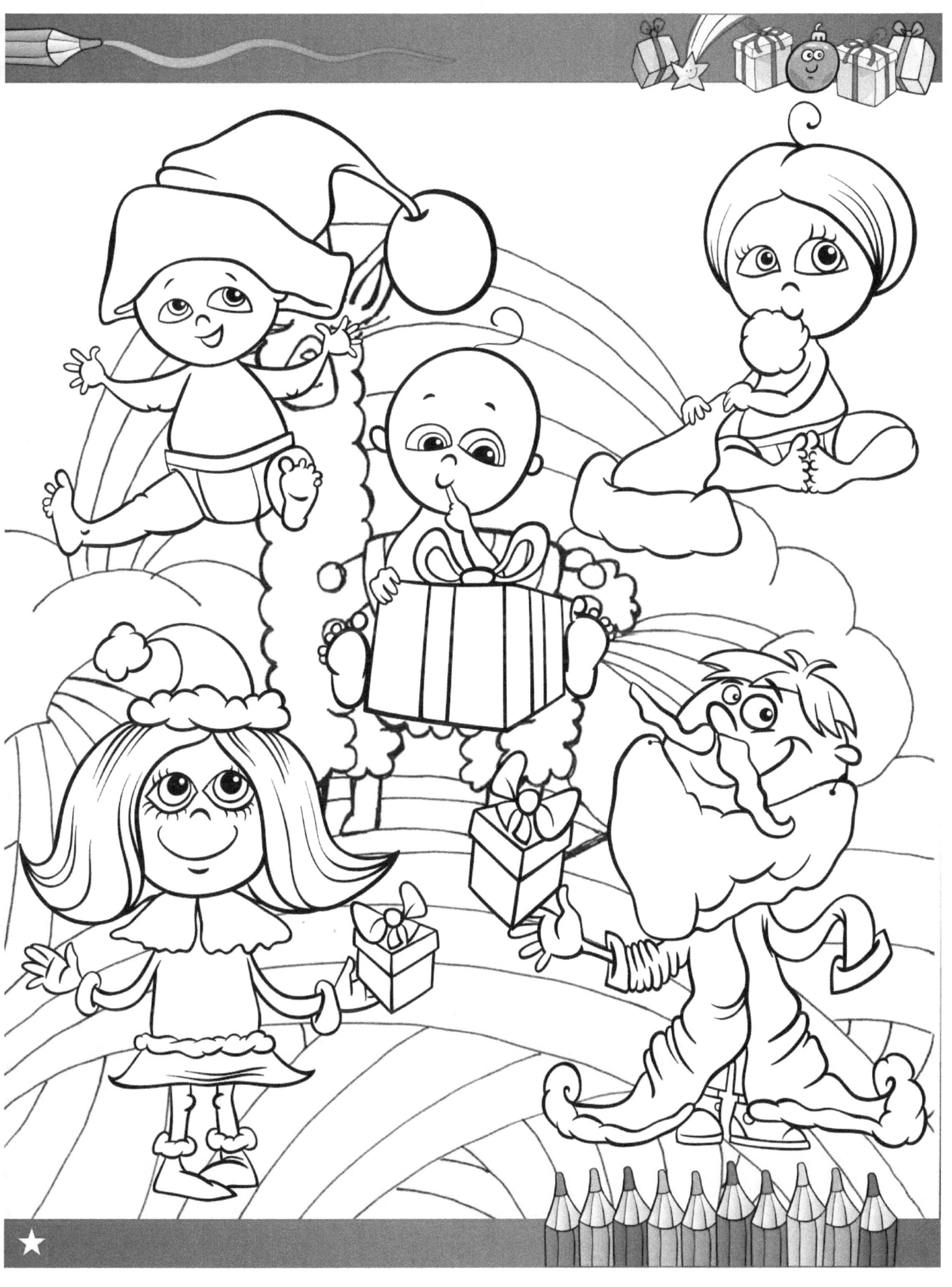

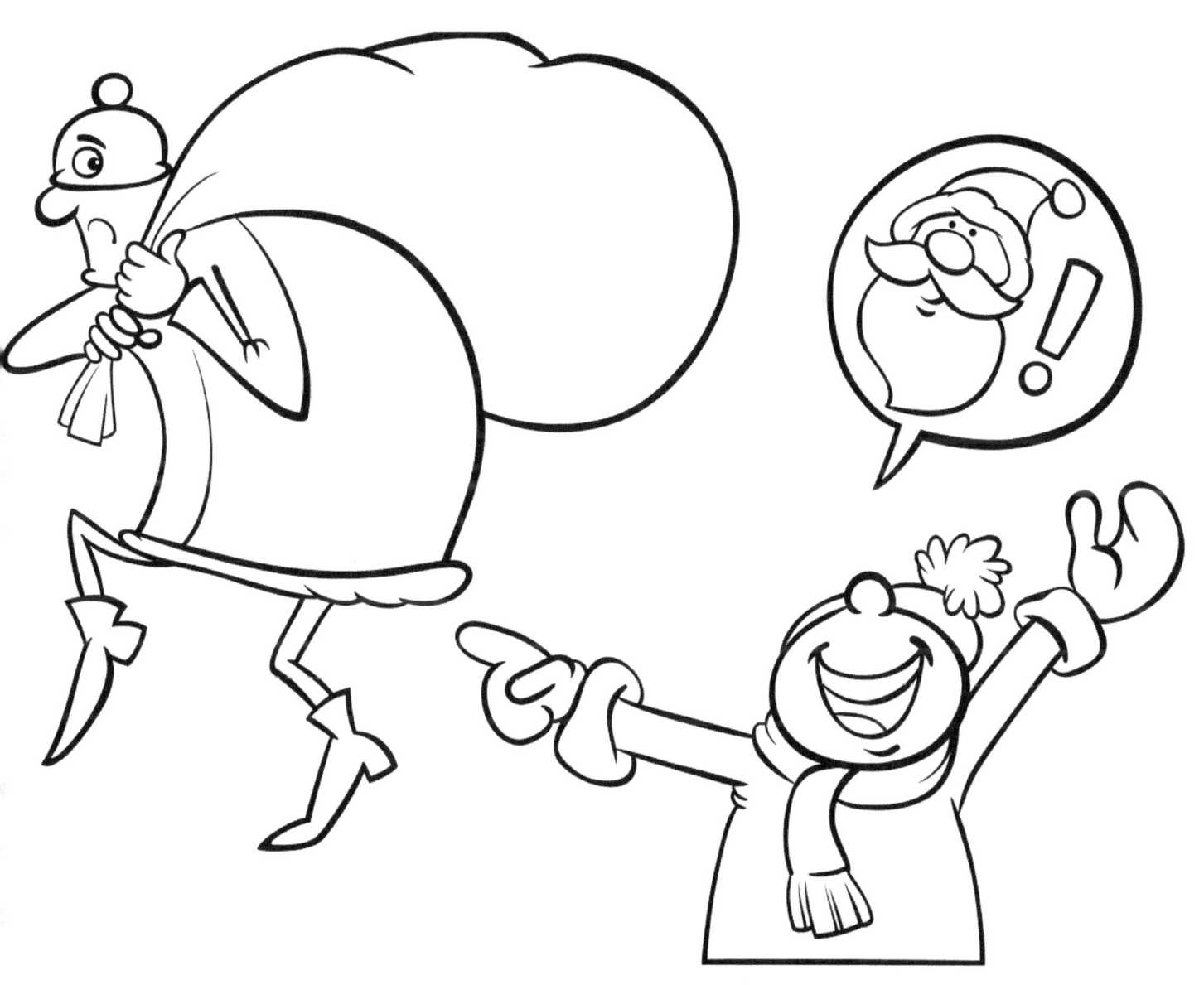

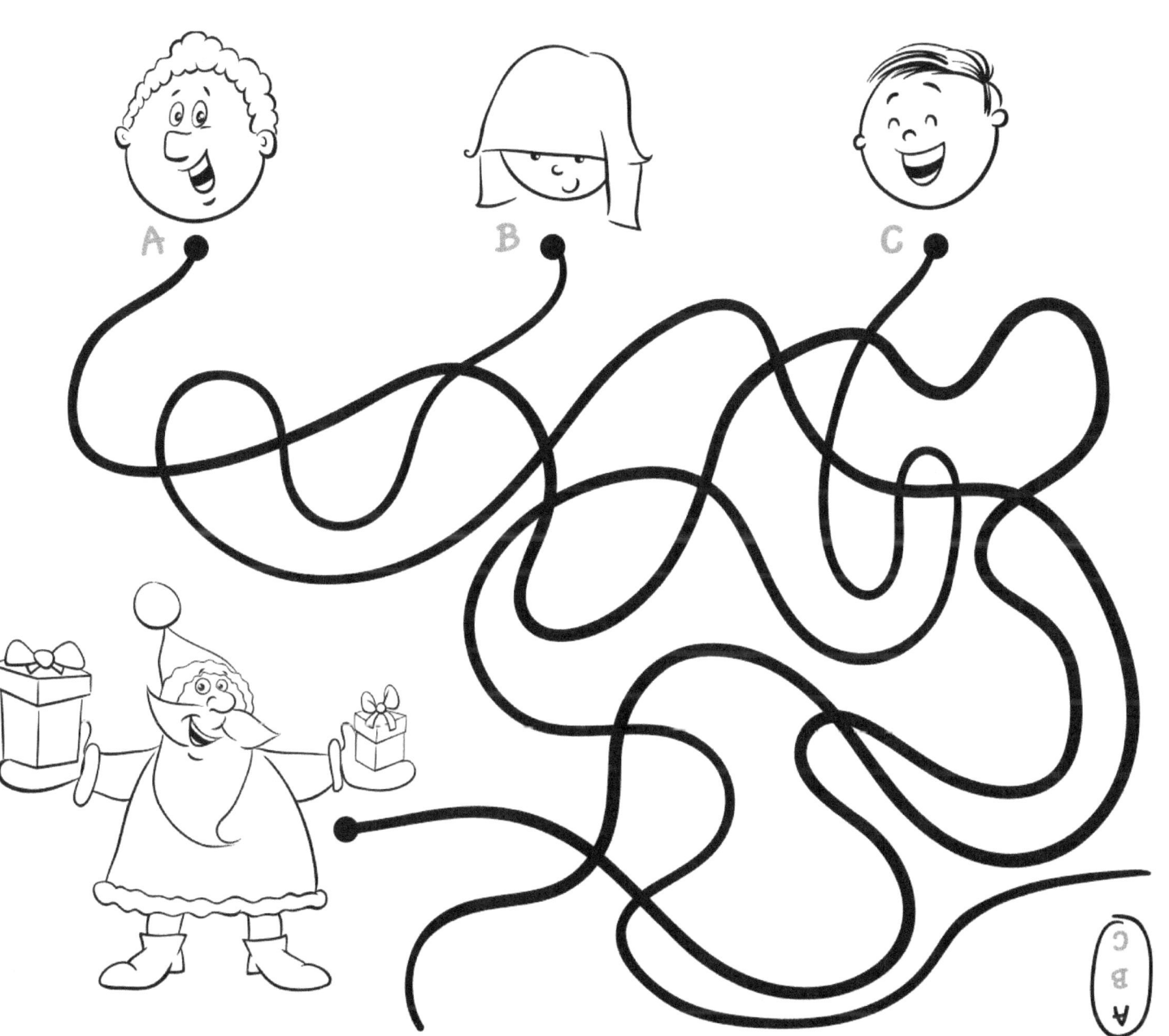

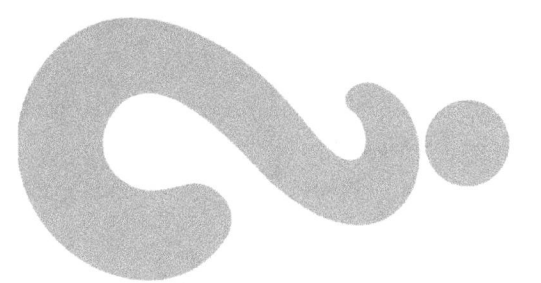
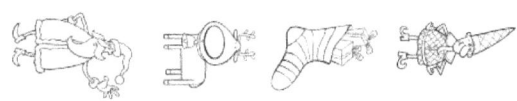

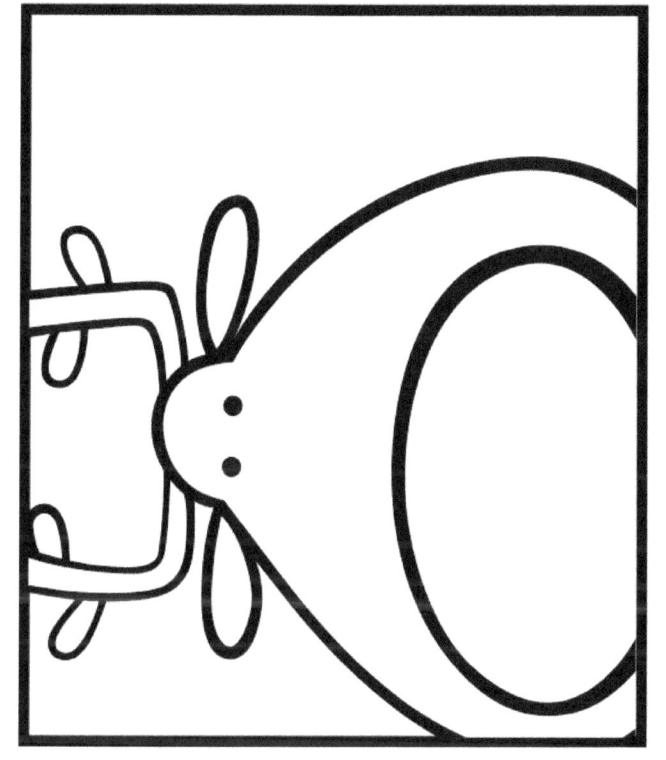
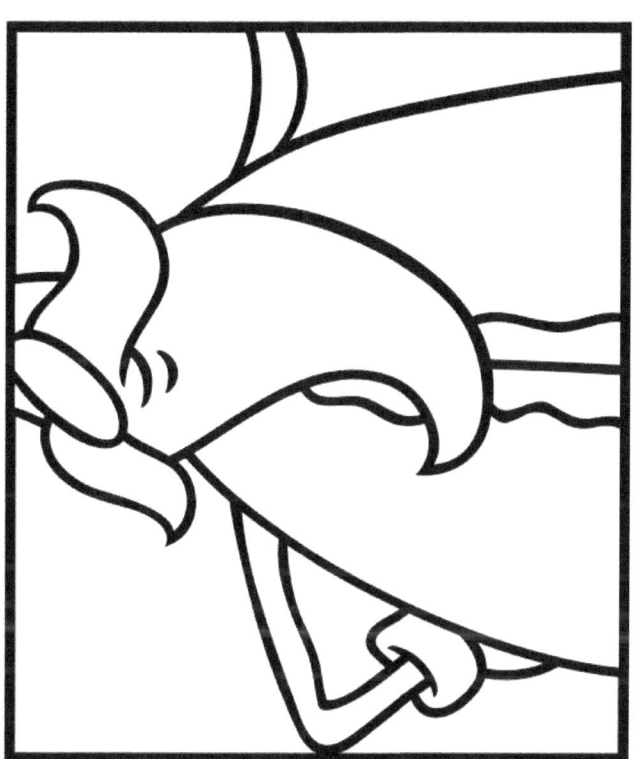
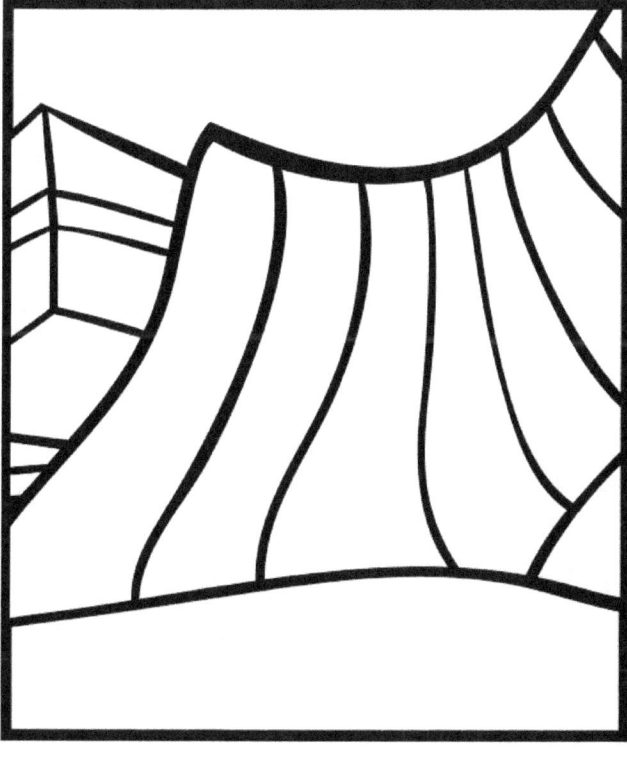
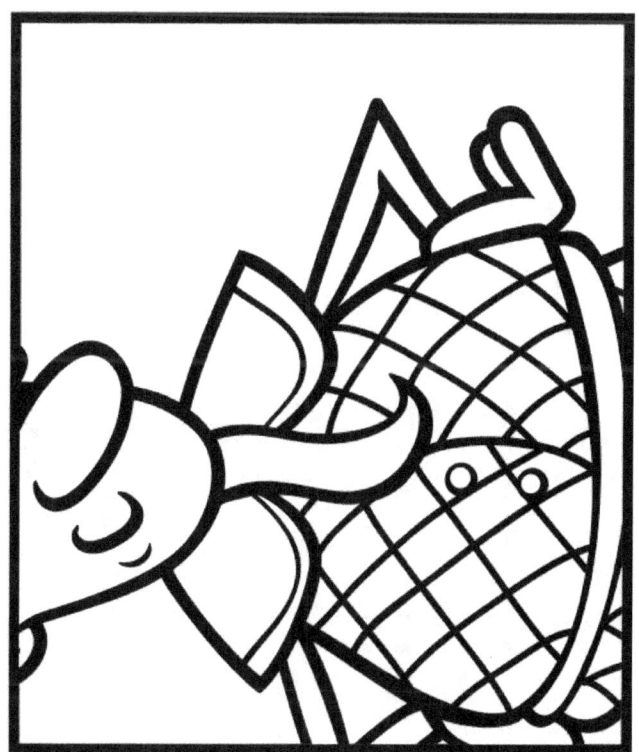

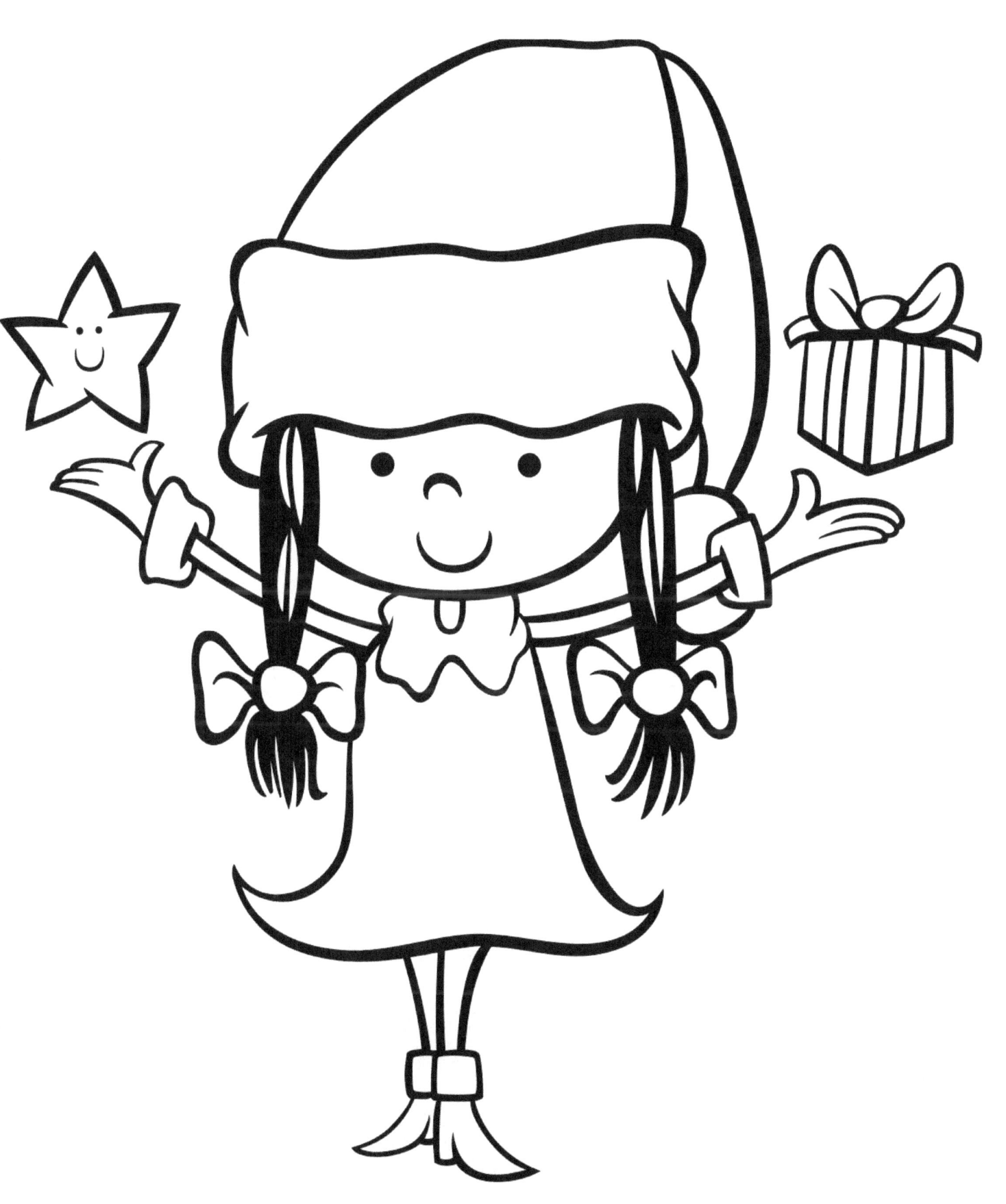

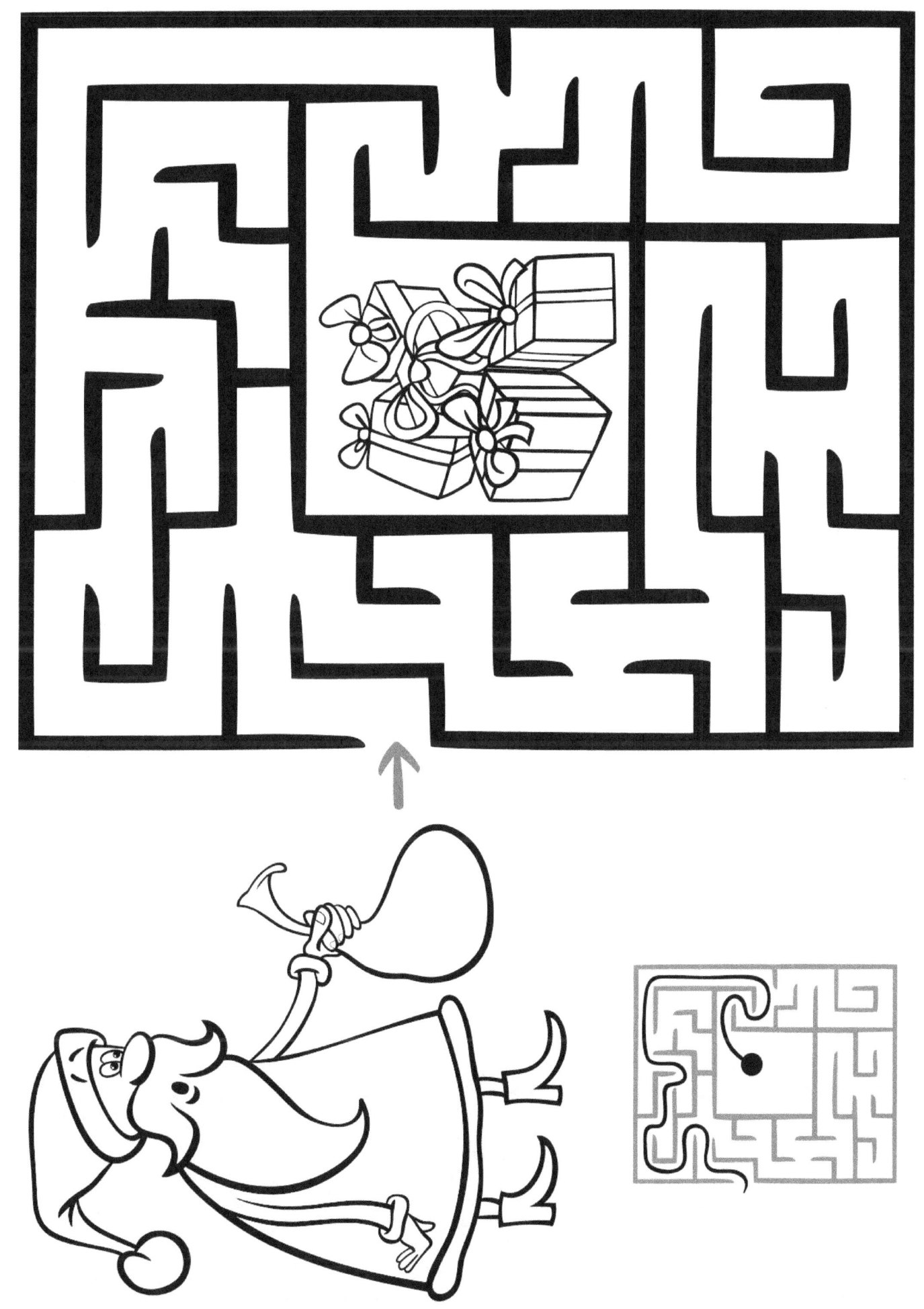

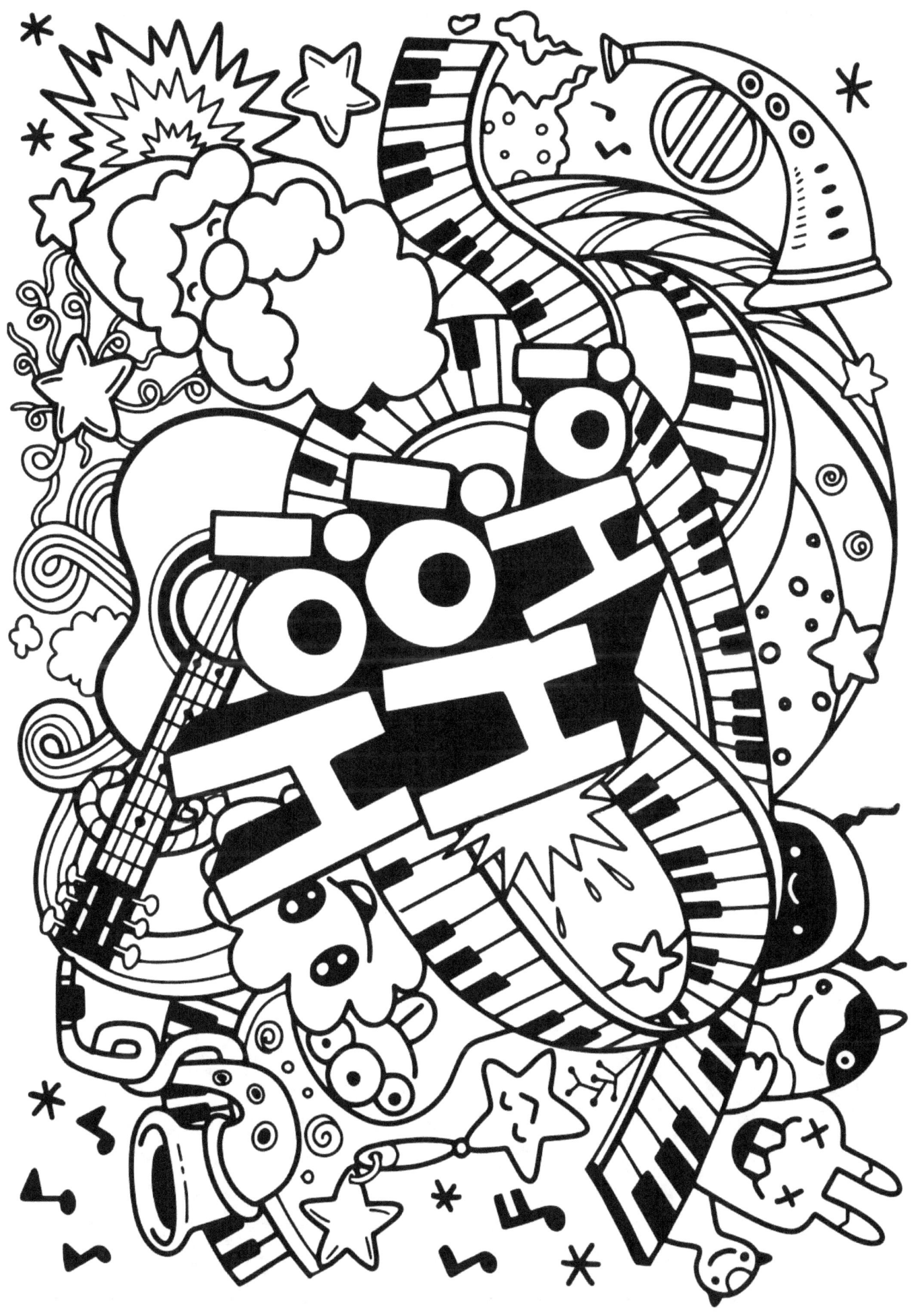

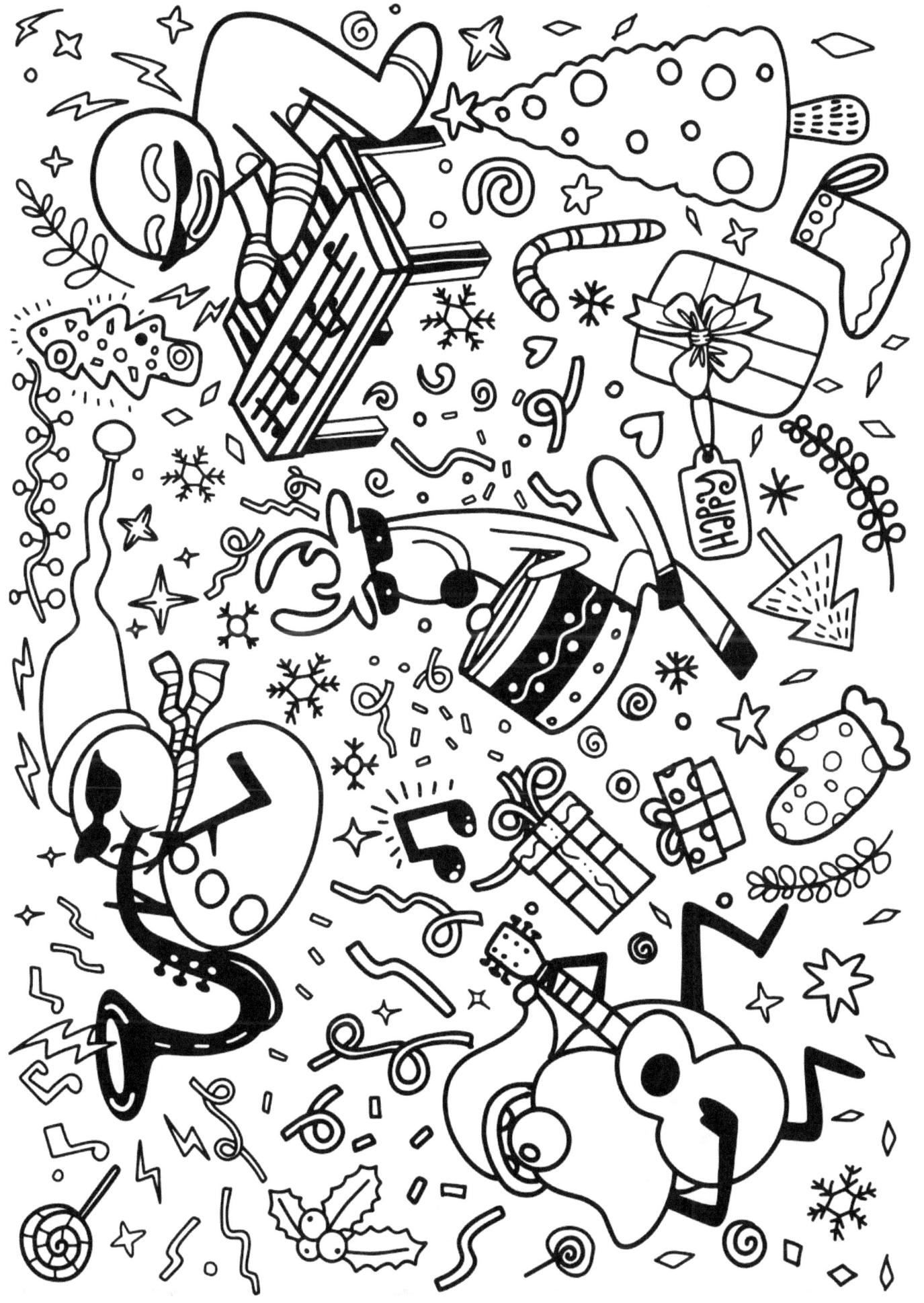

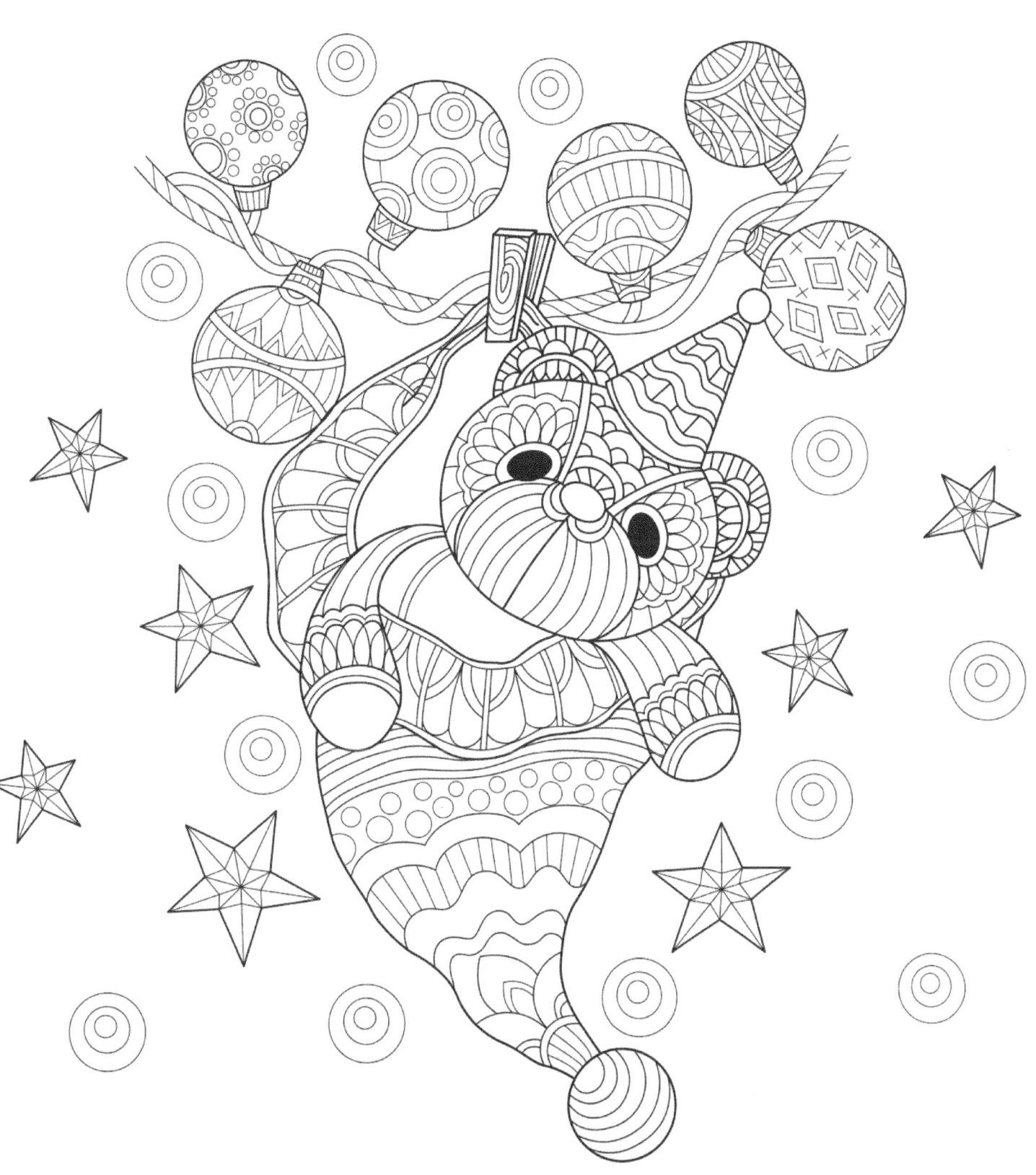

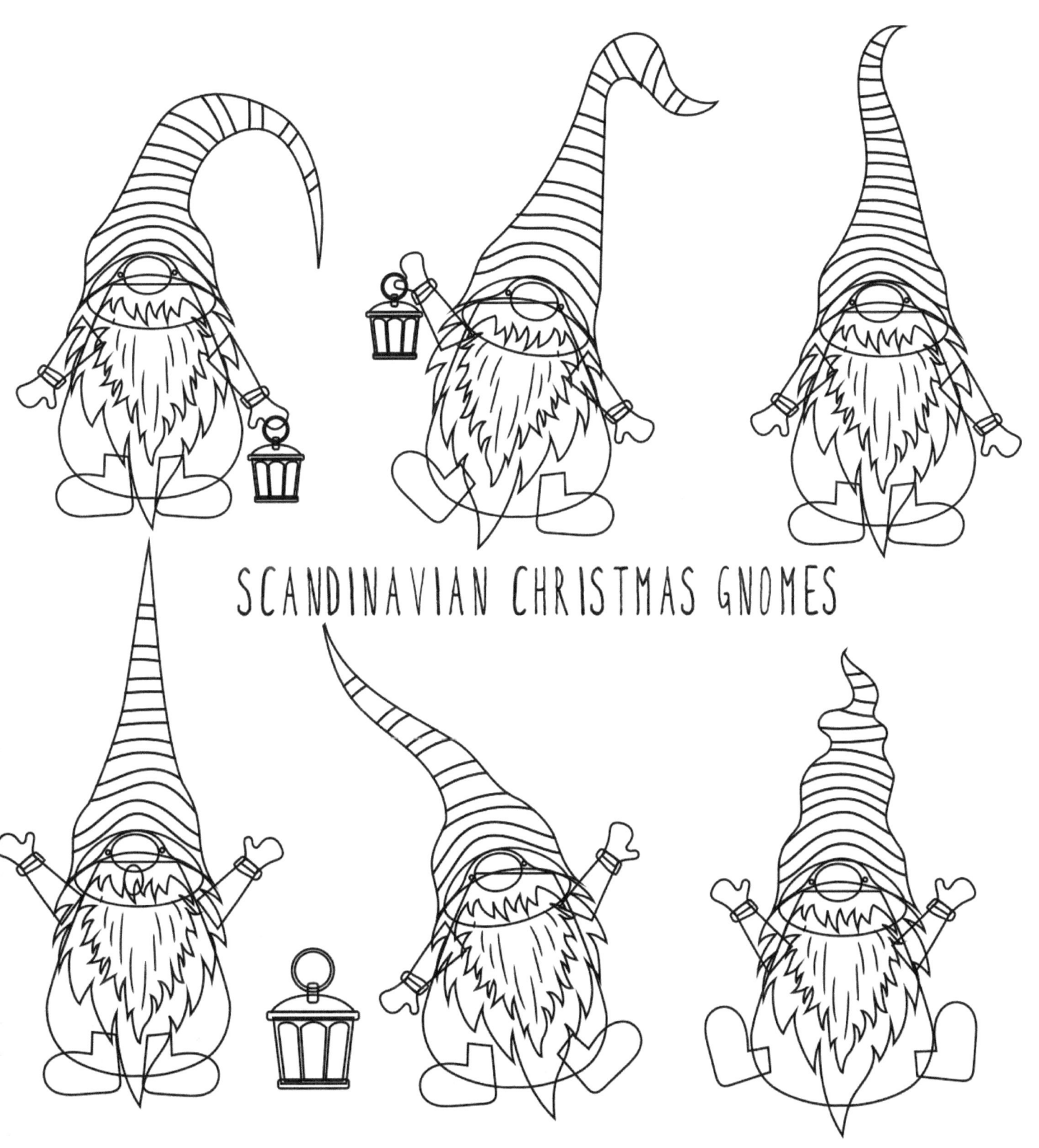

SCANDINAVIAN CHRISTMAS GNOMES

www.ingramcontent.com/pod-product-compliance
Lightning Source LLC
Chambersburg PA
CBHW081544220526
45467CB00010B/3317